SORT IT O... SIZE

By Emmett Alexander

Gareth Stevens
PUBLISHING

first
concepts

Sorting means putting things that are alike together. You can sort many things by size.

These boots are
different sizes.

These boots are
the same size.

These fish are
different sizes.

These fish are
the same size.

These dogs are
different sizes.

These dogs are small.

These flowers are
different sizes.

These flowers are tall.

These ladders are different sizes.

These ladders
are short.

These pumpkins are
different sizes.

These pumpkins are big.

These birds are different sizes.

These birds are little.

These buttons are
different sizes.

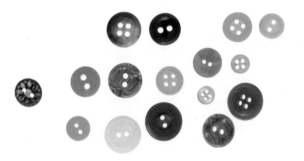

These buttons
are small.

These trees are
different sizes.

These trees are tall.

21

How would you sort
these gifts by size?

, www.garethstevens.com. For a free color catalog of all our high-quality
)0-542-2595 or fax 1-877-542-2596.

Library of Congress Cataloging-in-Publication Data

Alexander, Emmett.
Sort it by size / by Emmett Alexander.
p. cm. — (Sort it out!)
Includes index.
ISBN 978-1-4824-2573-4 (pbk.)
ISBN 978-1-4824-2574-1 (6 pack)
ISBN 978-1-4824-2575-8 (library binding)
1. Group theory — Juvenile literature. 2. Size perception — Juvenile literature. I. Title.
QA174.5 A449 2016
512—d23

First Edition

Published in 2016 by
Gareth Stevens Publishing
111 East 14th Street, Suite 349
New York, NY 10003

Copyright © 2016 Gareth Stevens Publishing

Designer: Sarah Liddell
Editor: Therese Shea

Photo credits: Cover, p. 1 (polka dots) Victoria Kalinina/Shutterstock.com; cover, p. 1 (buttons) Cre8tive Images/
Shutterstock.com; p. 3 hjschneider/Shutterstock.com; p. 4 RTimages/Shutterstock.com; p. 5 (left) HelenaQueen/
Shutterstock.com; p. 5 (right) Antonsov85/Shutterstock.com; p. 6 khz/Shutterstock.com; p. 7 Ljupco Smokovski/
Shutterstock.com; pp. 8, 9 (left), 16 (main) Eric Isselee/Shutterstock.com; p. 9 (middle) Felix Rohan/
Shutterstock.com; p. 9 (right) leungchopan/Shutterstock.com; p. 10 (flowers) vilax/Shutterstock.com;
pp. 10 (sunflowers), 11 Tsekhmister/Shutterstock.com; p. 12 Number 11/Shutterstock.com; p. 13 (left) Stephen
Coburn/Shutterstock.com; p. 13 (right) Elena Abduramanova/Shutterstock.com; p. 14 Jure Porenta/
Shutterstock.com; p. 15 TFoxFoto/Shutterstock.com; pp. 16 (chick), 17 Africa Studio/Shutterstock.com; p. 18 Garsya/
Shutterstock.com; p. 19 ludmilafoto/Shutterstock.com; p. 20 (left and right) Zerbor/Shutterstock.com; p. 20 (middle)
seeyou/Shutterstock.com; p. 21 (left) Muzhik/Shutterstock.com; p. 21 (middle) Eugene Sergeev/Shutterstock.com;
p. 21 (right) Iryna Rasko/Shutterstock.com; p. 23 Madlen/Shutterstock.com.

Printed in the United States of America

CPSIA compliance information: Batch #CS15GS: For further information contact Gareth Stevens, New York, New York at 1-800-542-2595.